The Big Laugh

I laugh,
You laugh,
We all laugh together;
Spring laugh,
Fall laugh,
A laugh for wintry weather;
Light laugh,
Dark laugh,
Night and morning laughter;
But it takes
The BIG laugh
To shake the roof and rafter.

Lee Blair

Little People™ Big Book

About
SILLY THINGS

ALEXANDRIA, VIRGINIA

Table of Contents

Funny People

Funny Animals

Funny World

Funny People

The Folk Who Live in Backward Town

The folk who live in Backward Town
Are inside out and upside down.
They wear their hats inside their heads
And go to sleep beneath their beds.
They only eat the apple peeling
And take their walks across the ceiling.

Mary Ann Hoberman

5

Seaside Limericks

There was an Old Man in a boat,
Who said, "I'm afloat! I'm afloat!"
    When they said, "No, you ain't!"
    He was ready to faint,
That unhappy Old Man in a boat.

Edward Lear

There was a Young Lady named Rose
Who was constantly blowing her nose;
    Because of this failing
    They sent her off whaling
So the whalers could say, "Thar she blows!"

William Jay Smith

There was an old man of Blackheath,
Who sat on his set of false teeth.
   Said he, with a start,
   "Oh my, bless my heart!
I've bitten myself underneath!"

Anonymous

There was an Old Man in a barge,
Whose nose was exceedingly large;
   But in fishing by night,
   It supported a light,
Which helped that Old Man in a barge.

Edward Lear

7

The Sillies

Q: Why did the Sillies run around their beds?
A: Because they wanted to catch up on their sleep.

Q: Why did Tilly Silly bring a ladder to class?
A: Because she was in high school.

Q: Why don't the Sillies use toothpaste?
A: Because their teeth aren't loose.

Q: Why did Billy Silly throw the clock out the window?
A: He wanted to see time fly.

Q: Why does Milly Silly keep her bicycle in the bedroom?
A: Because she's tired of walking in her sleep.

Q: Why is Mr. Silly tired of making faces?
A: Because he works in a clock factory.

Q: Why is Mrs. Silly knitting three socks?
A: Because Rilly Silly just wrote a letter from college to say he'd grown another foot.

The Funny Thing
by Wanda Ga'g

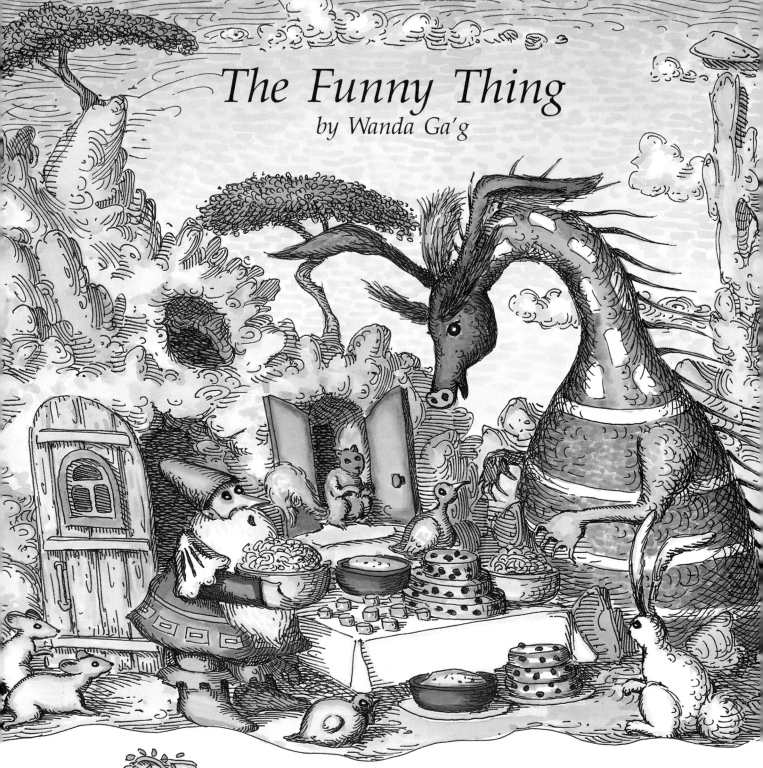

t was a beautiful day in the mountains. The sun was playing hide-and-seek among the fluffy, floating clouds, and the air was soft and warm.

Bobo, the good little man of the mountains, was waiting for the birds and animals to come. To come for what do you suppose? To come for food—because at the door of his mountain cave, Bobo had many good things for them to eat.

He had nut cakes for the fuzzy-tailed squirrels.

He had seed puddings for the pretty fluttering birds.

He had cabbage salads for the long-eared rabbits.

He had tiny cheeses—no bigger than cherries—and these were for the little mice.

Now on this beautiful sunny day, there came a Funny Thing which Bobo had never seen before. It looked something like a dog and also a little like a giraffe, and from the top of its head to the tip of its curled tail, there was a row of beautiful blue points.

"Good morning," said Bobo. "And what kind of animal are you?"

"I'm not an animal," said the Funny Thing. "I'm an *aminal!*"

Bobo was about to say there was no such word as *aminal*, when the Funny Thing looked around fiercely and cried, "And what have you for a hungry *aminal* to eat?"

"Oh," said Bobo, "here are some lovely nut cakes. I also have some fine seed puddings. This cabbage salad is very nice—and I'm sure you'd like these little cheeses."

But the Funny Thing turned away and said, "I never heard of such silly food! No *aminal* would eat those things. Haven't you any dolls today?"

"Dolls!" cried Bobo in surprise.

"Certainly," said the Funny Thing. "And very good they are— dolls."

"To eat?" cried Bobo, opening his eyes very wide at such an idea.

"To eat, of course," said the Funny Thing, smacking his lips. "And very good they are—dolls."

"But it is not kind to eat up little children's dolls," said Bobo. "I should think it would make them very unhappy."

"So it does," said the Funny Thing, smiling pleasantly, "but very good they are—dolls."

"And don't the children cry when you take away their dolls?" asked Bobo.

"Don't they though!" said the Funny Thing with a cheerful grin, "but very good they are—dolls."

Tears rolled down Bobo's face as he thought of the Funny Thing going around eating up dear little children's dolls.

"But perhaps you take only naughty children's dolls," he said, brightening up.

"No, I take them specially from good children," said the Funny Thing gleefully, "and *very* good they are—good children's dolls!"

"Oh, what shall I do?" thought Bobo, as he walked back and forth, back and forth. He was trying to think of a plan to make this naughty *aminal* forget to eat dolls.

At last he had an idea!

So he said to the Funny Thing, "What a lovely tail you have!"

The Funny Thing smiled and wriggled his tail with a pleased motion.

"And those pretty black eyebrows," Bobo continued.

The Funny Thing looked down modestly and smiled even more.

"But most wonderful of all is that row of blue points down your back," said Bobo.

The Funny Thing was so pleased that he rolled foolishly on the ground and smiled very hard.

Then Bobo, who was really a wise old man, said to the Funny Thing, "I suppose you are so beautiful because you eat a great many jum-jills?"

The Funny Thing had never heard of them.

"Jum-jills?" he asked eagerly. "What is a jum-jill—is it a kind of doll?"

"Oh no," said Bobo. "Jum-jills are funny little cakes which make blue points more beautiful, and little tails grow into big ones."

Now the Funny Thing was very vain and there was nothing he would rather have had than a very long tail and bigger and more beautiful blue points. So he cried, "Oh please, dear kind man, give me many jum-jills!"

"Very well," said Bobo. "Sit down under this tree and wait for me."

The Funny Thing was all smiles and did as he was told, while Bobo went into his cozy little home, which was like a sort of tunnel under the mountain.

First he had to go through his little bedroom. Next he came to his study and finally he reached the kitchen, where he usually made up the food for the birds and animals.

Now he took a big bowl, into which he put:

> seven nut cakes
> five seed puddings
> two cabbage salads
> and fifteen little cheeses.

He mixed them with a spoon and rolled them into little round balls.

These little balls were jum-jills.

He put them all on a plate and carried them out to the Funny Thing, who was still waiting under the tree.

"Here are your jum-jills," said Bobo, as he handed the plate to the Funny Thing.

The Funny Thing ate one and said, "And very good they are—jum-jills."

Then he ate another and said, "And very good they are—jum-jills."

And so on until he had eaten them all up.

"And *very* good they are—jum-jills," he said with a smack of his lips, after they were all gone.

Then the Funny Thing went home, but the next day he came back for more jum-jills. His tail was already a little longer, his blue points were beginning to grow, and he looked very happy indeed.

Every day the Funny Thing came back for more jum-jills. He came for a long, long time and each day his tail was a little longer. But on the twentieth day his tail had grown so long that he couldn't move about much.

So he chose a nice big mountain and sat on the very top of it. Every day Bobo sent birds to carry jum-jills to the Funny Thing, and as the Funny Thing's tail grew longer and longer, he curled it contentedly around his mountain.

His one joy in life was his beautiful blue-pointed tail, and by and by the only words he ever said were:

"And very good they are—jum-jills!"

So of course he ate no more dolls and we have kind old Bobo to thank for that.

A Funny Man

One day a funny kind of man
Came walking down the street.
He wore a shoe upon his head,
And hats upon his feet.

He raised the shoe and smiled at me,
His manners were polite;
But never had I seen before
Such a funny-sounding sight.

He said, "Allow me to present
Your Highness with a rose."
And taking out a currant bun
He held it to my nose.

I staggered back against the wall,
And then I answered, "Well!
I never saw a rose with such
A funny-looking smell."

He then began to sing a song,
And sat down on the ground;
You never heard in all your life
Such a funny-feeling sound.

"My friend, why do you wear two hats
Upon your feet?" I said.
He turned the other way about,
And hopped home on his head.

Natalie Joan

16

Jilliky Jolliky Jelliky Jee

Jilliky Jolliky Jelliky Jee,
three little cooks in a coconut tree,
one cooked a peanut and one cooked a pea,
one brewed a thimble of cinnamon tea,
then they sat down to a dinner for three,
Jilliky Jolliky Jelliky Jee.

Jack Prelutsky

There Was an Old Man with a Beard

There was an Old Man with a beard,
Who said, "It is just as I feared!—
Two Owls and a Hen, four Larks and a Wren,
Have all built their nests in my beard!"

Edward Lear

Funny
Animals

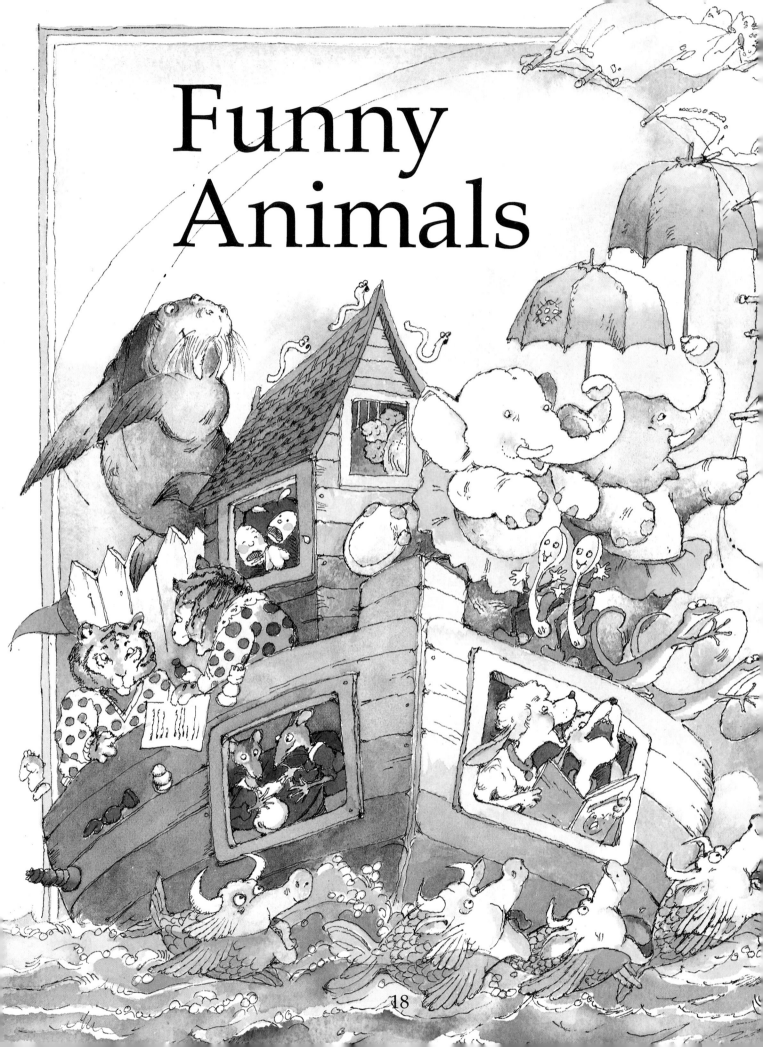

Nonsense!

Nonsense? That's what makes no sense;
a walrus waltzing on a fence,
cats in vats of cheese and chowder,
weasels sniffing sneezing powder,
elephants with bright umbrellas
dancing sprightly tarantellas,
tigers dressed in spotted sweaters
playing chess and writing letters.

Nonsense? Lizards clanging cymbals,
flying eggs and weeping thimbles,
sleeping prunes and crooning poodles,
hopping spoons and creeping noodles,
schools of fish that moo like cattle,
bloomers marching into battle,
pigs with wigs and purple wings.
Nonsense! All these silly things.

Jack Prelutsky

The Forgetful Bears
by Lawrence Weinberg

ne spring morning Mrs. Forgetful woke up and went to the window.

"What a beautiful day," she said. "Wake up everyone. Let's go to the country and have a picnic."

"Hooray!" shouted Sally and Tommy Forgetful. "We'll make the lemonade."

They ran to the kitchen, and squeezed lots of lemons. They added sugar. They added water. Soon the lemonade was ready. But they forgot about the picnic and drank it all themselves.

"I'll wake up Grandpa," said Mr. Forgetful. But he forgot where Grandpa's room was and walked into a closet. There on the shelf was his bowler hat.

"Just what I'm looking for!" he said, and put it on. Then he closed the door behind him and forgot to come out.

Soon Mrs. Forgetful was ready to leave. "All right, everybody," she called. "Let's go!" But she forgot where the front door was.

Instead she opened the door to the closet.

"Ah, there you are!" said Mr. Forgetful, who was standing inside. "Have you forgotten that we're going on a picnic?"

At last the four Forgetfuls found their way out of the house. They piled into their car and drove off.

Suddenly Mrs. Forgetful cried out, "Turn back! I forgot the food!"

Mr. Forgetful headed back for town. But he forgot what street they lived on and couldn't find the house.

Finally Mr. Forgetful suggested they look for their house on foot. They walked up one street and down another.

"There's our house," cried Tommy Forgetful.

"No! Our house is red," said Sally Forgetful.

"Hmmm. I thought it was blue," said Mr. Forgetful.

"Well, maybe we've moved," said Mrs. Forgetful. "I'm tired. Let's go back to the car."

But where was the car? Nobody could remember.

Tommy Forgetful had a bright idea. "Let's split up," he said. "Each bear will walk in a different direction. The first bear to find the car will honk the horn and let the rest of us know where it is."

And so the four Forgetful Bears went on their separate ways.

Mrs. Forgetful walked down a street where there were many stores. A supermarket sign said, "Big Sale Today." She forgot about the car, and hurried inside to shop.

Sally Forgetful walked down another street where there was a park. She forgot about the car, and sat down to rest.

Tommy Forgetful came to a bus stop. He forgot about the car and hopped on a bus.

Mr. Forgetful kept walking and walking. He forgot about the car and walked straight out of town.

Meanwhile, Grandpa Forgetful woke up. He rubbed his eyes and got out of bed. "Where is everybody?" he shouted. He went outside

23

to look. There, across the street, was the family car.

"What luck," said Grandpa. And he drove off to find the other Forgetfuls.

Soon he saw Sally Forgetful, asleep on a bench. "Poor child, she's tired," he said to himself. He stopped and carried Sally to the back seat of the car.

A little while later Grandpa saw Mrs. Forgetful leaving the supermarket. "Poor woman, she sure is loaded down," he said. He took some of her packages and helped her into the car.

Grandpa stopped for a light and saw Tommy Forgetful. "Poor boy, why is he riding on the bus?" Grandpa honked the horn. "Come with us, Tommy."

So Tommy hopped off the bus and slid in next to Grandpa. "Where are we going?" Tommy asked.

"It's such a nice day," Grandpa said. "How would you like to go for a picnic in the country?"

"What a wonderful idea!" said Mrs. Forgetful. "Why didn't *I* think of that?"

So they drove out into the country. Along the road they spotted Mr. Forgetful, walking *very* slowly. Grandpa stopped the car. "Poor man! You look tired. Hop in!" he said.

"Thank you," Mr. Forgetful said. "But I never accept rides from strangers."

"But we're your FAMILY!" shouted Mrs. Forgetful. "I'm your wife and this is your son and this is your daughter and this is your *father!*"

"Well, in that case," said Mr. Forgetful, "I guess I will get in the car. But don't tell me your names. I'm sure they will come to me."

So they drove to a lovely spot by the river. They made sandwiches from the groceries Mrs. Forgetful had bought. And they all had a wonderful time—which they never forgot.

Farm Funnies to Make You Hee-Hee-Haw

Q: How many sides does a barn have?
A: Two—inside and outside.

Q: What do you call a sleeping bull?
A: A bull-dozer.

Q: Which animal is best at spelling?
A: A bee.

Q: Why do cows wear bells?
A: Their horns don't work.

Q: What does a sheep have that no other animal has?
A: Lambs.

Q: Why are fish so well educated?
A: They're always found in schools.

Q: What makes more noise than a rooster?
A: Two roosters.

Q: Why does a dog wag his tail?
A: Because no one else will wag it for him.

Q: Why do hummingbirds hum?
A: Because they don't know the words.

Crocodile

The Crocodile wept bitter tears,
  And when I asked him why,
He said: "I weep because the years
  Go far too quickly by!

"I weep because of oranges,
  I weep because of pears,
Because of broken door hinges,
  And dark and crooked stairs.

"I weep because of black shoestrings,
  I weep because of socks,
I weep because I can't do things
  Like dance and shadowbox.

"I weep because the deep blue sea
   Washes the sand in a pile;
I weep because, as you can see,
   I've never learned to smile!"

"To weep like that cannot be fun,
   My reptile friend," I said;
"Your nose, though long, will run
   and run,
Your eyes, though wide, be red.

"Why must you so give way to grief?
   You *could* smile if you chose;
Here, take this pocket handkerchief
   And wipe your eyes and nose.

"Come, laugh because of oranges,
   And laugh because of pears,
Because of broken door hinges,
   And dark and crooked stairs.

"Come, laugh because of black shoestrings,
   And laugh because of socks,
And laugh because you *can* do things
   Like dance and shadowbox.

"Come, laugh because it feels so good—
   It's not against the law.
Throw open, as a reptile should,
   Your green and shining jaw!"

The Crocodile he thought awhile
   Till things seemed not so black;
He smiled, and I returned his smile,
   He smiled, and I smiled back.

30

He took an orange and a pear;
    He took shoestrings and socks,
And tossing them into the air,
    Began to waltz and box.

The animals came, and they were gay:
    The Bobcat danced with the Owl;
The Bat brought tea on a bamboo tray
    To the Yak and the Guinea Fowl.

The Monkeys frolicked in the street;
    The Lion, with a smile,
Came proudly down the steps to greet
    The happy Crocodile!

William Jay Smith

Blue Moose

by Manus Pinkwater

 r. Breton had a little restaurant on the edge of the big woods. When winter came, the north wind blew through the trees and froze everything solid. Then it snowed. Mr. Breton didn't like it.

Mr. Breton was a very good cook. Every day people from the town came to his restaurant. They ate gallons of his special clam chowder. They ate plates of his special beef stew. They ate fish stew and special homemade bread. The people from the town never talked much, and they never said anything about Mr. Breton's cooking.

"Did you like your clam chowder?" Mr. Breton would ask.

"Yup," the people from the town would say.

Mr. Breton wished they would say, "Delicious!" or "Good chowder, Breton!" All they ever said was, "Yup." In winter they came on skis and snowshoes.

Every morning Mr. Breton went out behind his house to get firewood. He wore three sweaters, a scarf, galoshes, a woolen hat, a big checkered coat, and mittens. He still felt cold. Sometimes raccoons and rabbits came out of the woods to watch Mr. Breton. The cold didn't bother them. It bothered Mr. Breton even more when they watched him.

One morning there was a moose in Mr. Breton's yard. It was a blue moose. When Mr. Breton went out his back door, the moose was there, looking at him. After a while Mr. Breton went back in and made a pot of coffee while he waited for the moose to go away. It didn't go away; it just stood in Mr. Breton's yard, looking at his back door. Mr. Breton drank a cup of coffee. The moose stood in the yard. Mr. Breton opened the door again. "Shoo! Go away!" he said to the moose.

"Do you mind if I come in and get warm?" said the moose. "I'm just about frozen." He brushed past Mr. Breton and walked into the kitchen. His antlers almost touched the ceiling.

The moose sat down on the floor next to Mr. Breton's stove. He closed his eyes and sat leaning toward the stove for a long time. Wisps of steam began to rise from his blue fur. After a long time the moose sighed. It sounded like a foghorn.

"Can I get you a cup of coffee?" Mr. Breton asked the moose. "Or some clam chowder?"

"Clam chowder," said the moose.

Mr. Breton filled a bowl with creamy clam chowder and set it on the floor. The moose dipped his big nose into the bowl and snuffled up the chowder. He made a sort of slurping, whistling noise.

"Sir," the moose said, "this is wonderful clam chowder."

Mr. Breton blushed a very deep red. "Do you really mean that?"

"Sir," the moose said, "I have eaten some very good chowder in my time, but yours is the very best."

"Oh my," said Mr. Breton, blushing even redder. "Oh my. Would you like some more?"

"Yes, with crackers," said the moose.

The moose ate seventeen bowls of chowder with crackers. Then he had twelve pieces of hot gingerbread and forty-eight cups of coffee. While the moose slurped and whistled, Mr. Breton sat in a chair. Every now and then he said to himself, "Oh my. The best he's ever eaten. Oh my."

Later, when some people from the town came to Mr. Breton's house, the moose met them at the door. "How many in your party, please?" the moose asked. "I have a table for you; please follow me."

The people from the town were surprised to see the moose. They felt like running away, but they were too surprised. The moose led them to a table, brought them menus, looked at each person, snorted, and clumped into the kitchen. "There are people outside; I'll take care of them," he told Mr. Breton.

The people were whispering to one another about the moose when he clumped back to the table. "Are you ready to order?" he asked.

"Yup," said the people from the town. They waited for the moose to ask them if they would like some chowder, the way Mr. Breton always did. But the moose just stared at them as though they were very foolish. The people felt uncomfortable. "We'll have the clam chowder."

"Chaudière de clam; very good," the moose said. "Do you desire crackers or homemade bread?"

"We will have crackers," said the people from the town.

"I suggest you have the bread; it is hot," said the moose.

"We will have bread," said the people from the town.

"And for dessert," said the moose, "will you have fresh gingerbread or apple jacquette?"

"What do you recommend?" asked the people from the town.

"After the chaudière de clam, the gingerbread is best."

"Thank you," said the people from the town.

"It is my pleasure to serve you," said the moose. He brought bowls of chowder balanced on his antlers.

At the end of the meal, the moose clumped to the table. "Has everything been to your satisfaction?"

"Yup," said the people from the town, their mouths full of gingerbread.

"I beg your pardon?" said the moose. "What did you say?"

"It was very good," said the people from the town. "It was the best we've ever eaten."

"I will tell the chef," said the moose.

The moose clumped into the kitchen and told Mr. Breton what the people from the town had said. Mr. Breton rushed out of the kitchen and out of the house. The people from the town were sitting on the porch, putting on their snowshoes.

"Did you tell the moose that my clam chowder was the best you've ever eaten?" Mr. Breton asked.

"Yup," said the people from the town. "We said that. We think that you are the best cook in the world; we have always thought so."

"Always?" asked Mr. Breton.

"Of course," the people from the town said. "Why do you think we walk seven miles on snowshoes just to eat here?"

The people from the town walked away on their snowshoes. Mr. Breton sat on the edge of the porch and thought it over. When the moose came out to see why Mr. Breton was sitting outside without his coat on, Mr. Breton said, "Do you know, those people think I am the best cook in the whole world?"

"Of course they do," the moose said. "By the way, aren't you cold out here?"

"No, I'm not the least bit cold," Mr. Breton said. "This is turning out to be a very mild winter."

When spring finally came, the moose became moody. He spent a lot of time staring out the back door. Flocks of geese flew overhead, returning to lakes in the north, and the moose always stirred when he heard their honking.

"Chef," said the moose one morning, "I will be going tomorrow. I wonder if you would pack some gingerbread for me to take along."

Mr. Breton baked a special batch of gingerbread, packed it in parcels, and tied the parcels with string so the moose could hang them from his antlers. When the moose came downstairs, Mr. Breton was sitting in the kitchen, drinking coffee. The parcels of gingerbread were on the kitchen table.

"Do you want a bowl of coffee before you go?" Mr. Breton asked.

"Thank you," said the moose.

"I shall certainly miss you," Mr. Breton said.

"Thank you," said the moose.

"You are the best friend I have," said Mr. Breton.

"Thank you," said the moose.

"Do you suppose you'll ever come back?" asked Mr. Breton.

"Not before Thursday or Friday," said the moose. "It would be impolite to visit my uncle for less than a week." The moose hooked his antlers into the loops of string on the parcels of gingerbread. "My uncle will like this." He stood up and turned toward the door.

"Wait!" Mr. Breton shouted. "Do you mean that you are not leaving forever? I thought you were lonely for the life of a wild moose. I thought you wanted to go back to the wild free places."

"Chef, do you have any idea how cold it gets in the wild free places?" the moose said. "And the food! Terrible!"

"Have a nice time at your uncle's," said Mr. Breton.

"I'll send you a postcard," said the moose.

Funny World

On the Ning Nang Nong

On the Ning Nang Nong
Where the Cows go Bong!
And the Monkeys all say Boo!
There's a Nong Nang Ning
Where the trees go Ping!
and the tea pots Jibber Jabber Joo.
On the Nong Ning Nang
All the mice go Clang!
And you just can't catch 'em when they do!
So it's Ning Nang Nong!
Cows go Bong!
Nong Nang Ning!
Trees go Ping!
Nong Ning Nang!
The mice go Clang!
What a noisy place to belong,
Is the Ning Nang Ning Nang Nong!!

Spike Milligan

41

Foolish Questions

Where can a man buy a cap for his knee?
Or a key for the lock of his hair?
And can his eyes be called a school?
I would think—there are pupils there!
What jewels are found in the crown of his head,
And who walks on the bridge of his nose?
Can he use, in building the roof of his mouth,
The nails on the ends of his toes?
Can the crook of his elbow be sent to jail—
If it can, well, then, what did it do?
And how does he sharpen his shoulder blades?
I'll be hanged if I know—do you?
Can he sit in the shade of the palm of his hand,
And beat time with the drum in his ear?
Can the calf of his leg eat the corn on his toe?—

There's somethin' pretty strange around here!

American Folk Rhyme,
adapted by William Cole

42

HEE HEE HEE

Have You Ever Seen?

Have you ever seen a sheet on a river bed?
Or a single hair from a hammer's head?
Has the foot of a mountain any toes?
And is there a pair of garden hose?

Does the needle ever wink its eye?
Why doesn't the wing of a building fly?
Can you tickle the ribs of a parasol?
Or open the trunk of a tree at all?

Are the teeth of a rake ever going to bite?
Have the hands of a clock any left or right?
Can the garden plot be deep and dark?
And what is the sound of the birch's bark?

Anonymous

A Nonsense Alphabet

A was once an apple pie,
  Pidy,
    Widy,
      Tidy,
        Pidy,
Nice insidy,
Apple pie!

B was once a little bear,
  Beary,
    Wary,
      Hairy,
        Beary,
Taky cary,
Little bear!

C was once a little cake,
  Caky,
    Baky,
      Maky,
        Caky,
Taky caky,
Little cake!

D was once a little doll,
  Dolly,
    Molly,
      Polly,
        Nolly,
Nursy dolly,
Little doll!

E was once a little eel,
  Eely,
    Weely,
      Peely,
        Eely,
Twirly tweely,
Little eel!

F was once a little fish,
  Fishy,
    Wishy,
      Squishy,
        Fishy,
In a dishy,
Little fish!

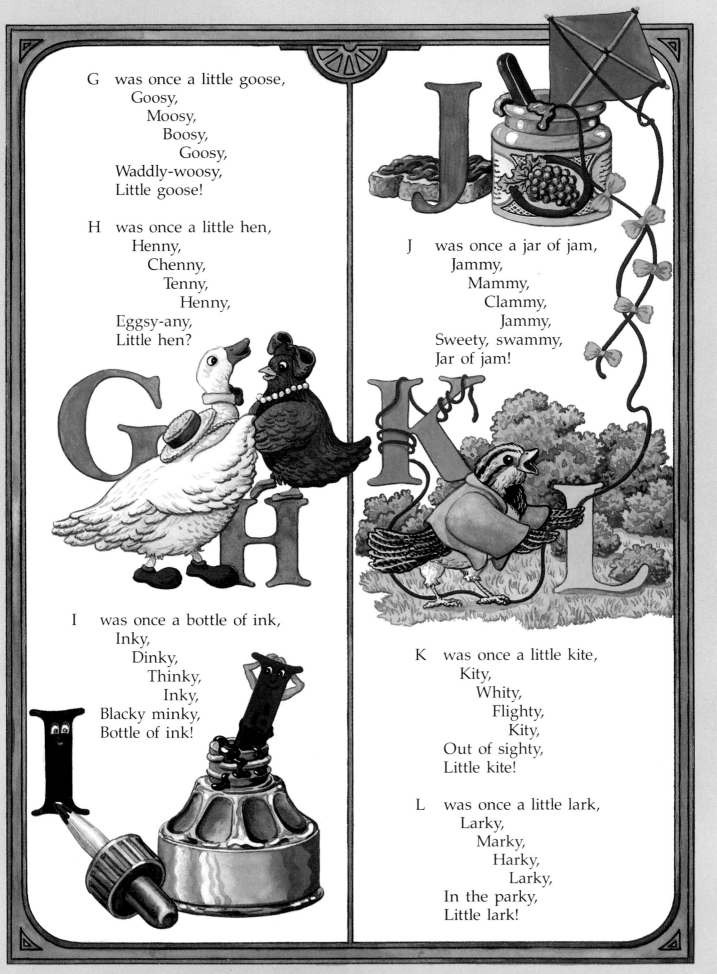

G   was once a little goose,
    Goosy,
      Moosy,
        Boosy,
          Goosy,
    Waddly-woosy,
    Little goose!

H   was once a little hen,
    Henny,
      Chenny,
        Tenny,
          Henny,
    Eggsy-any,
    Little hen?

I   was once a bottle of ink,
    Inky,
      Dinky,
        Thinky,
          Inky,
    Blacky minky,
    Bottle of ink!

J   was once a jar of jam,
    Jammy,
      Mammy,
        Clammy,
          Jammy,
    Sweety, swammy,
    Jar of jam!

K   was once a little kite,
    Kity,
      Whity,
        Flighty,
          Kity,
    Out of sighty,
    Little kite!

L   was once a little lark,
    Larky,
      Marky,
        Harky,
          Larky,
    In the parky,
    Little lark!

M was once a little mouse,
    Mousy,
      Bousy,
        Sousy,
          Mousy,
In the housy,
Little mouse!

N was once a little needle,
    Needly,
      Tweedly,
        Threedly,
          Needly,
Wisky, wheedly,
Little needle!

O was once a little owl,
    Owly,
      Prowly,
        Howly,
          Owly,
Browny, fowly,
Little owl!

P was once a little pump,
    Plumpy,
      Slumpy,
        Flumpy,
          Pumpy,
Dumpy, thumpy,
Little pump!

Q was once a little quail,
    Quaily,
      Faily,
        Daily,
          Quaily,
Stumpy-taily,
Little quail!

R was once a little rose,
    Rosy,
      Posy,
        Nosy,
          Rosy,
Blows-y, grows-y,
Little rose!

S was once a little shrimp,
    Shrimpy,
      Nimpy,
        Flimpy,
          Shrimpy,
Jumpy, jimpy,
Little shrimp!

T   was once a little thrush,
        Thrushy,
            Hushy,
                Bushy,
                    Thrushy,
    Flitty, flushy,
    Little thrush!

U   was once a little urn,
        Urny,
            Burny,
                Turny,
                    Urny,
    Bubbly, burny,
    Little urn!

V   was once a little vine,
        Viny,
            Winy,
                Twiny,
                    Viny,
    Twisty-twiny,
    Little vine!

W   was once a whale,
        Whaly,
            Scaly,
                Shaly,
                    Whaly,
    Tumbly-taily,
    Mighty whale!

X   was once a great king Xerxes,
        Xerxy,
            Perxy,
                Turxy,
                    Xerxy,
    Linky, lurxy,
    Great King Xerxes!

Y   was once a little yew,
        Yewdy,
            Fewdy,
                Crudy,
                    Yewdy,
    Growdy, grewdy,
    Little yew!

Z   was once a piece of zinc,
        Tinky,
            Winky,
                Blinky,
                    Tinky,
    Tinkly minky,
    Piece of zinc!

Edward Lear

47

Bring On the Clowns!

Bring on the clowns!
Bring on the clowns!
Clowns wearing knickers
and clowns
wearing gowns.

Tall clowns and short clowns and skinny and fat,
a flat-footed clown with a jumping-jack hat.
A clown walking under a portable shower,
getting all wet just to water a flower.
A barefoot buffoon with balloons on his toes,
a clown with a polka-dot musical nose.
Clowns wearing teapots and clowns sporting plumes,
a clown with a tail made of brushes and brooms.

A balancing clown on a wobbly wheel,
seventeen clowns in an automobile.
Two jesters on pogo sticks dressed up in kilts,
pursuing a prankster escaping on stilts.
A sad-looking clown with a face like a tramp,
a clown with his stomach lit up like a lamp.
How quickly a clown can coax smiles out of frowns!
Make way for the merriment . . . bring on the clowns!

Jack Prelutsky

DID YOU EVER WONDER
ABOUT CIRCUS CLOWNS

What do clowns wear?
Clowns wear colorful costumes and use silly props to entertain their audiences. Here are some of them:

funny hat

curly wig

rubber nose

colorful shirt

face makeup

alarm-clock wristwatch

flower that squirts water

flowered tie

long, long hanky

white gloves

giant lollipop

baggy pants

big, floppy shoes

How do clowns learn to be funny?
They go to clown school! Young clowns learn skills like juggling and acrobatics. They learn to walk on stilts and to ride a unicycle. They perform silly skits using different props and costumes. Clowns have to pass a "funny test" before they go to work in a circus.

How does a clown put on makeup?
Each clown has his or her own special clown face. It may take a few years of practice before a beginning clown designs just the right face. When a clown decides how to paint his face, he keeps the same face for the rest of his career. No other clown uses that face, even when the clown retires.

Washes face to make sure it's clean.

Puts on white greasepaint.

Adds colorful lines and dots to cheeks and eyes.

Paints on a big smile.

What tricks can animal clowns do?
Animal trainers work patiently with the circus animals to teach them how to do tricks. Dogs learn to jump through hoops. Chimpanzees learn to roller-skate and to drive pedal cars. Seals learn to balance and toss balls. Bears are slow to learn, but they can be taught to ride unicycles. Sometimes animal clowns perform in skits with the other clowns. All the animal clowns wear colorful costumes.

If We Walked on Our Hands

If we walked on our hands
   instead of our feet
And we all ate paper
   instead of meat
What a mixed-up place this world would be.
What a mixed-up
   fixed-up
   topsy-turvy
   sit-u-a-tion.

If we wore our hats
   on our behinds
And all we ate
   were melon rinds
What a mixed-up place this world would be.
What a mixed-up
   fixed-up
   topsy-turvy
   sit-u-a-tion.

If babies worked
   while papas played
If the children gave orders
   and parents obeyed
What a mixed-up place this world would be.
What a mixed-up
   fixed-up
   topsy-turvy
   sit-u-a-tion.

Beatrice Schenk de Regniers

Purple

If purple was the only color in the world . . .
You would read about "Snow Purple and The Seven Dwarfs."
You would sing about
   "The Purple Grass Growing All Around, All Around,"
And you would drink purple juice for breakfast.
You'd write with chalk on the purpleboard,
And cross the street when the light turned purple,
And visit the President of the United States in the Purple House.
You could even write a poem that begins:
   Roses are purple, violets are purple . . .
It's a good thing there are other colors.

Jeff Moss

Cloudy with a Chance of Meatballs

by Judi Barrett

We were all sitting around the big kitchen table. It was Saturday morning. Pancake morning. Mom was squeezing oranges for orange juice. Henry and I were betting on how many pancakes we each could eat. And Grandpa was doing the flipping.

Seconds later, something flew through the air headed toward the kitchen ceiling . . . and landed right on Henry.

After we realized that the flying object was only a pancake, we all laughed, even Grandpa. Breakfast continued quite uneventfully. All the other pancakes landed in the pan. And all of them were eaten, even the one that landed on Henry.

That night, touched off by the pancake incident at breakfast, Grandpa told us the best tall-tale bedtime story he'd ever told.

"Across an ocean, over lots of huge bumpy mountains, across three hot deserts, and one smaller ocean . . . there lay the tiny town of Chewandswallow.

In most ways, it was very much like any other tiny town. It had a Main Street lined with stores, houses with trees and gardens around them, a schoolhouse, about three hundred people, and some assorted cats and dogs.

But there were no food stores in the town of Chewandswallow. They didn't need any. The sky supplied all the food they could possibly want.

The only thing that was really different about Chewandswallow was its weather. It came three times a day, at breakfast, lunch, and dinner. Everything that everyone ate came from the sky.

Whatever the weather served, that was what they ate.

But it never rained rain. It never snowed snow. And it never blew just wind. It rained things like soup and juice. It snowed mashed potatoes and green peas. And sometimes the wind blew in storms of hamburgers.

The people could watch the weather report on television in the morning and they would even hear a prediction for the next day's food.

When the townspeople went outside, they carried their plates, cups, glasses, forks, spoons, knives, and napkins with them. That way they would always be prepared for any kind of weather.

If there were leftovers, and there usually were, the people took them home and put them in their refrigerators in case they got hungry between meals.

The menu varied.

By the time they woke up in the morning, breakfast was coming down.

After a brief shower of orange juice, low clouds of sunnyside-up eggs moved in followed by pieces of toast. Butter and jelly sprinkled down for the toast. And most of the time it rained milk afterwards.

For lunch one day, frankfurters, already in their rolls, blew in from the northwest at about five miles an hour.

There were mustard clouds nearby. Then the wind shifted to the east and brought in baked beans.

A drizzle of soda finished off the meal.

Dinner one night consisted of lamb chops, becoming heavy at times, with occasional ketchup. Periods of peas and baked potatoes were followed by gradual clearing, with a wonderful Jell-O setting in the west.

The Sanitation Department of Chew-andswallow had a rather unusual job for a sanitation department. It had to remove the food that fell on the houses and sidewalks and lawns. The workers cleaned things up after every meal and fed all the dogs and cats. Then they emptied some of it into the surrounding oceans for the fish and turtles and whales to eat. The rest of the food was put back into the earth so that the soil would be richer for the people's flower gardens.

Life for the townspeople was delicious until the weather took a turn for the worse.

One day there was nothing but Gorgonzola cheese all day long.

The next day there was only broccoli, all overcooked.

And the next day there were brussel sprouts and peanut butter with mayonnaise.

Another day there was a pea soup fog. No one could see where they were going, and they could barely find the rest of the meal that got stuck in the fog.

The food was getting larger and larger, and so were the portions. The people were getting frightened. Violent storms blew up frequently. Awful things were happening.

One Tuesday there was a hurricane of bread and rolls all day long and into the night. There were soft rolls and hard rolls, some with seeds and some without. There was white bread and rye and whole wheat toast. Most of it was larger than they had ever seen bread and rolls before. It was a terrible day. Everyone had to stay indoors. Roofs were damaged, and the Sanitation Department was beside itself. The mess took the workers four days to clean up, and the sea was full of floating rolls.

To help out, the people piled up as much bread as they could in their backyards. The birds picked at it a bit, but it just stayed there and got staler and staler.

There was a storm of pancakes one morning and a downpour of maple syrup that nearly flooded the town. A huge pancake covered the school. No one could get it off because of its weight, so they had to close the school.

Lunch one day brought fifteen-inch drifts of cream cheese and jelly sandwiches. Everyone ate themselves sick and the day ended with a stomachache.

There was an awful salt-and-pepper wind accompanied by an even worse tomato tornado. People were sneezing themselves silly and running to avoid the tomatoes. The town was a mess. There were seeds and pulp everywhere.

The Sanitation Department gave up. The job was too big.

Everyone feared for their lives. They couldn't go outside most of the time. Many houses had been badly damaged by giant meatballs, stores were boarded up and there was no more school for the children.

So a decision was made to abandon the town of Chewandswallow.

It was a matter of survival.

The people glued together the giant pieces of stale bread sandwich-style with peanut batter . . . took the absolute necessities with them, and set sail on their rafts for a new land.

After being afloat for a week, they finally reached a small coastal town, which welcomed them. The bread had held up surprisingly well, well enough for them to build temporary houses for themselves out of it.

The children began school again, and the adults all tried to find places for themselves in the new land. The biggest change they had to make was getting used to buying food at a supermarket. They found it odd that the food was kept on shelves, packaged in boxes, cans, and bottles. Meat that had to be cooked was kept in large refrigerators. Nothing came down from the sky except rain and snow. The clouds above their heads were not made of fried eggs. No one ever got hit by a hamburger again.

And nobody dared to go back to Chewandswallow to find out what had happened to it. They were too afraid."

Henry and I were awake until the very end of Grandpa's story. I remember his good-night kiss.

The next morning we woke up to see snow falling outside our window.

We ran downstairs for breakfast and ate it a little faster than usual so we could go sledding with Grandpa.

It's funny, but even as we were sliding down the hill we thought we saw a giant pat of butter at the top, and we could almost smell mashed potatoes.

61

MIXED-UP FAIRY TALES

*These fairy-tale characters have gotten into the wrong stories!
Look at the silly mix-ups. Then, tell how the stories really
should be.*

The glass slipper was a perfect fit on Pinocchio's foot.
Whenever Cinderella didn't tell the truth, her nose grew
several inches longer.

"I made the bread myself and I'll eat it myself," said Red
Riding Hood. The Little Red Hen carried a basket of
goodies to Grandma's house.

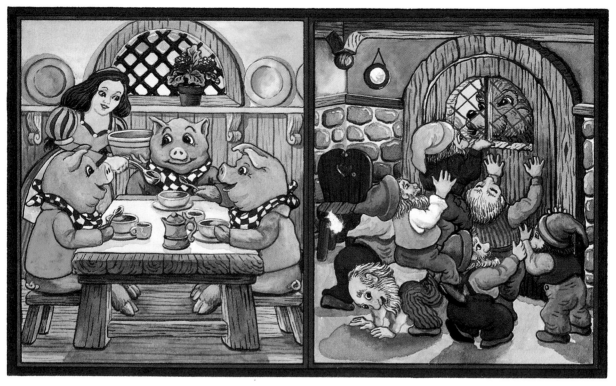

Snow White kept house for the Three Little Pigs. The Big Bad Wolf huffed and puffed at the door of the Seven Dwarfs.

A tiny pea under the bottom mattress kept the Three Bears awake all night. The Princess came home and found that someone had eaten her porridge.

Little People™ Big Book About SILLY THINGS

TIME-LIFE for CHILDREN™

Publisher: Robert H. Smith
Managing Editor: Neil Kagan
Editorial Directors: Jean Burke Crawford,
              Patricia Daniels, Karin Kinney
Editorial Coordinator: Elizabeth Ward
Marketing Director: Ruth P. Stevens
Product Manager: Margaret Mooney
Production Manager: Prudence G. Harris
Administrative Assistant: Rebecca C. Christoffersen
Editorial Consultants: Jacqueline A. Bell, Sara Mark

PRODUCED BY PARACHUTE PRESS, INC.

Editorial Director: Joan Waricha
Editors: Christopher Medina, Jane Stine, Wendy Wax
Writer: Carol Sumerel
Designer: Greg Wozney
Illustrators: Shirley Beckes (p. 6-7, 26-27), Debbie
          Dieneman (p. 20-25), Joan Holub
          (p. 52-53), John O'Brien (p. 10-15, 42-43),
          Carol Schwartz (p. 44-47, 62-63),
          Gill Speirs (endpapers), John Speirs
          (cover, p. 4-5, 18-19, 40-41, 50-51, 54-61),
          John Wallner (p. 8-9, 16-17, 32-39),
          Linda Weller (p. 28-31, 48-49)

Time-Life Books Inc. is a wholly owned subsidiary of THE TIME INC. BOOK COMPANY.

TIME-LIFE is a trademark of Time Warner Inc. U.S.A.

FISHER-PRICE, LITTLE PEOPLE and AWNING DESIGN are trademarks of Fisher-Price, Division of The Quaker Oats Company, and are used under license.

Time-Life Books Inc. offers a wide range of fine publications, including home video products. For subscription information, call 1-800-621-7026, or write TIME-LIFE BOOKS, P.O. Box C-32068, Richmond, Virginia 23261-2068.

ACKNOWLEDGMENTS

Every effort has been made to trace the ownership of all copyrighted material and to secure the necessary permissions to reprint these selections. If any question arises as to the use of any material, the editor and the publisher, while expressing regret for any inadvertent error, will make the necessary correction in future printings.

Grateful acknowledgment is made to the following for permission to reprint copyrighted material: Bantam Books, a division of Bantam, Doubleday, Dell for US/Canadian rights to "Purple" from THE BUTTERFLY JAR by Jeff Moss. Copyright © 1989 by Jeff Moss. William Cole for "Foolish Questions." Greenwillow Books, a div. of William Morrow, for "Jilliky Jolliky Jelliky Jee" from RIDE A PURPLE PELICAN by Jack Prelutsky. Copyright © 1986 by Jack Prelutsky. Farrar, Straus & Giroux for "Crocodile" and "There was a Young Lady named Rose" from LAUGHING TIME by William Jay Smith. Copyright © 1955, 1957, 1980, 1990 by William Jay Smith. International Creative Management for British rights to "Purple" from THE BUTTERFLY JAR by Jeff Moss. Copyright © 1989 by Jeff Moss. Gina Maccoby Literary Agency for "The Folk Who Live in Backward Town" from HELLO AND GOOD-BY by Mary Ann Hoberman. Copyright © 1959, renewed 1987 by Mary Ann Hoberman. Macmillan Publishing Co. for CLOUDY WITH A CHANCE OF MEATBALLS by Judi Barrett. Copyright © 1978 by Judi Barrett, reprinted with permission of Atheneum Publishers, an imprint of Macmillan; and "Bring On The Clowns!" from CIRCUS by Jack Prelutsky. Copyright © 1974 by Jack Prelutsky. Spike Milligan Productions Ltd. for "On The Ning, Nang, Nong" from SILLY VERSE FOR KIDS by Spike Milligan. Published by Puffin Books. Oak Tree Publications, Inc. for "A Funny Man" by Natalie Joan from BARNES BOOK OF NURSERY VERSE. Putnam Publishing Group for THE FUNNY THING by Wanda Ga'g. Copyright © 1929 by Wanda Ga'g, renewed 1957 by Robert Janssen; and BLUE MOOSE by Manus Pinkwater. Copyright © 1975 by Manus Pinkwater. Random House, Inc. for "Nonsense" from THE RANDOM HOUSE BOOK OF POETRY FOR CHILDREN selected and introduced by Jack Prelutsky. Copyright © 1983 by Random House, Inc. Marion Reiner for "If We Walked on Our Hands" from SOMETHING SPECIAL by Beatrice Schenk de Regnier. Copyright © 1958, 1986 by Beatrice Schenk de Regnier. Scholastic, Inc. for THE FORGETFUL BEARS by Lawrence Weinberg. Copyright © 1981 by Lawrence Weinberg. Published by arrangement with Scholastic, Inc.

The Big Laugh

I laugh,
You laugh,
We all laugh together;
Spring laugh,
Fall laugh,
A laugh for wintry weather;
Light laugh,
Dark laugh,
Night and morning laughter;
But it takes
The BIG laugh
To shake the roof and rafter.

Lee Blair